11-9-06   Smart   Apple/Bond $ $33.⁰⁰

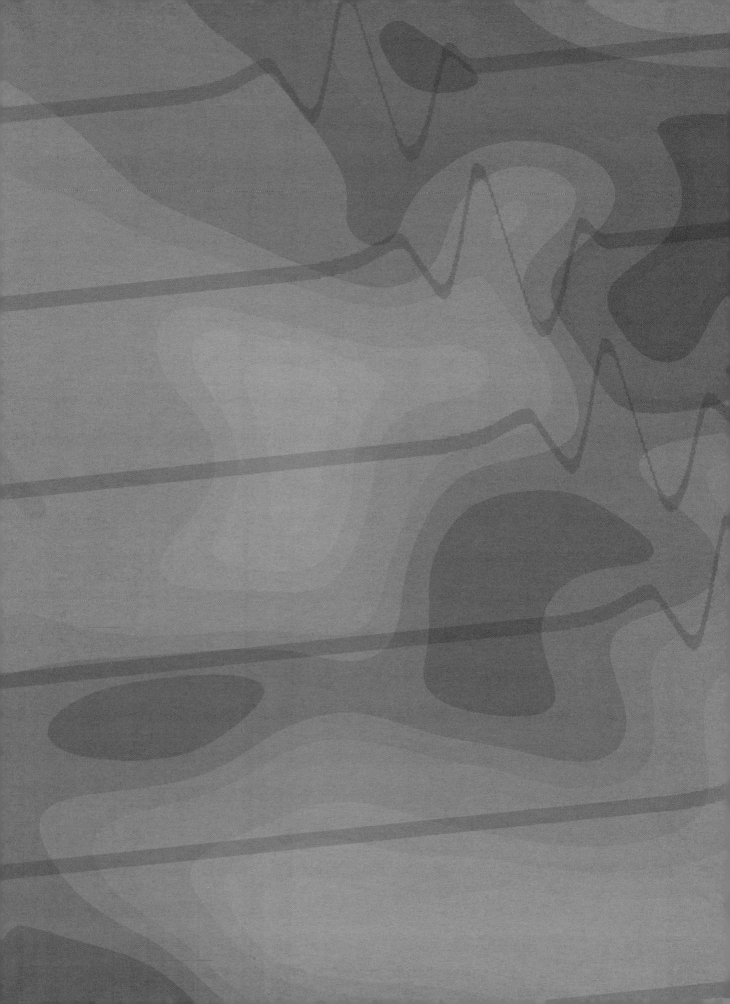

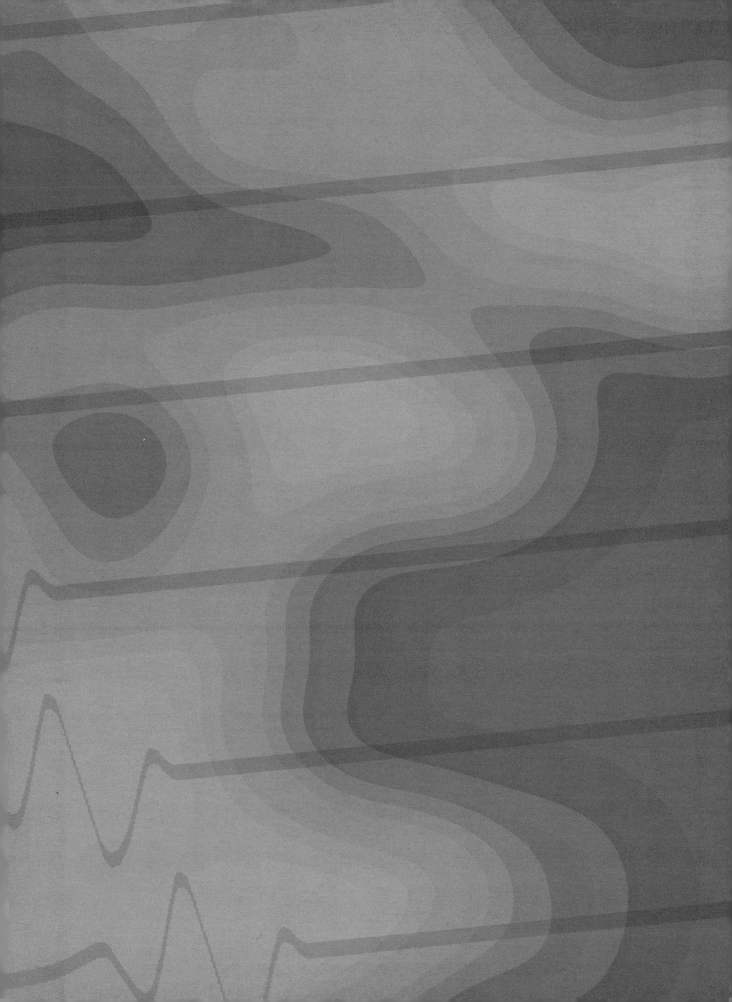

Smart Apple/Bound $

It's Your Health!

Self–esteem

JILLIAN POWELL

A+
Smart Apple Media

First published in 2004 by Franklin Watts
96 Leonard Street, London EC2A 4XD

Franklin Watts Australia
45–51 Huntley Street, Alexandria NSW 2015

Series editor: Sarah Peutrill, Editor: Sarah Ridley, Designed by: Pewter Design Associates, Series design: Peter Scoulding, Picture researcher: Sophie Hartley, Series consultant: Wendy Anthony, Health Education Unit, Education Service, Birmingham City Council

Picture credits: © Paul Baldesare/Photofusion: 16, 22, 24, 27t, 36t. © Joe Bator/Corbis: 15b. © Bettmann/Corbis: 9t. Photo from www.JohnBirdsall.co.uk: 23b. Brand X Pictures/Alamy: 41. © Robert Brook/Photofusion: 32b. Peter Brooker/Rex Features: 29t. © Graham Burns/Photofusion: 38. © Jacky Chapman/Photofusion: 14, 30b. Crollalanza/Rex Features: 12. Chris Fairclough/Franklin Watts: 4, 11t, 11b, 17b, 17t, 19b, 20, 21, 23t, 37b, 45. FBA/Rex Features: 32t. © Melanie Friend/Photofusion: 31. © Raymond Gehman/Corbis: 39b. Gusto/Science Photo Library: 25b. © Debbie Humphry/Photofusion: 28. Ali Kabas/Alamy: 40. © Reed Kaestner/Corbis: 13b. © Ute Klaphake/Photofusion: 25t. © Clarissa Leahy/Photofusion: 10. © Colin McPherson/Corbis: 35. Ray Moller/Franklin Watts: 36b. Jeff Morgan/Alamy: 33. © Jose Luis Pelaez, Inc./Corbis: 9b. © Michael Pole/Corbis: 34. © Rob & Sas/Corbis: 37t. © Norbert Schaefer/Corbis: 19t. © Paula Solloway/Photofusion: 18. © Tom Stewart/Corbis: 27b. Vinnie Suffante/Rex Features: 30t. Topham Picturepoint: 29b. © David Tothill/Photofusion: 39t. U.S. National Institute of Health/Science Photo Library: 26. © Bob Watkins/Photofusion: 15t. Janine Wiedel Photolibrary/Alamy: 8. World Religions Photo Library/Alamy: 13t.

Published in the United States by Smart Apple Media
2140 Howard Drive West, North Mankato, Minnesota 56003

U.S. publication copyright © 2006 Smart Apple Media

Library of Congress Cataloging-in-Publication Data

Powell, Jillian.
Self-esteem / by Jillian Powell.
p. cm. — (It's your health)
Includes index.
ISBN 1-58340-589-5
1. Self-esteem—Juvenile literature. I. Title. II. Series.

BF697.5.S46P69 2005
158.1—dc22   2004057853

9 8 7 6 5 4 3 2 1

Contents

What is self-esteem?

Self-esteem is how we think and feel about ourselves. It refers to how we think about the way we look, our abilities, our relationships with others, and our hopes for the future. We are not born with self-esteem—it is something we develop as we get older.

All of these teenagers look as if they are having a good time, but it is difficult to know what is really going on inside other people's heads. We need to develop a positive inner voice and try not to base our happiness on other people's feelings about us.

Opinion, not fact

Self-esteem is based on our inner feelings, not on facts. Research has shown that there is often a wide gap between how we are seen and how we think we are seen. Self-esteem can be an important factor in our lives. It can affect our health, our career decisions, our relationships, and the way we deal with problems we may have to face, such as bullying or peer pressure. Self-esteem is an important factor in making us feel happy.

It's your experience

"I'm always talking to myself in my head, saying, 'You made a mess of that, you shouldn't have worn that.... 'It's like I'm really down on myself."

Kate, age 17

American psychologist William James (1842-1910).

Social identity

Psychologists have been studying self-esteem since William James first wrote about it more than 100 years ago. He wrote about our ideas of self and social identity—how we see ourselves in relation to a wider society or community.

Today, many workplaces and schools work to improve the self-esteem of their employees or students. They believe that we can only respect others if we respect ourselves. If we have a sense of our own worth, we are more likely to value others and act responsibly toward them.

It is good to be realistic about our own abilities so that we can feel positive about results, knowing we have tried our hardest.

It's your decision

Do you let your imperfections take over? It is normal to like and dislike some things about yourself. But this doesn't make you any less likeable or worthwhile as a person.

Respect!

Having high self-esteem means we feel positive about ourselves as individuals and in comparison to others. It means that we value our strengths and feel like we are in control of our lives and our futures. With high self-esteem, we see the world as a good place full of friends and people who respond positively to us.

How do we get self-esteem?

Self-esteem begins to be formed when we are babies. If someone feeds us and cuddles us when we cry, we feel that we are loved and valued. We begin to trust our parents or guardians, knowing that they keep us safe and well. As we get older, we look to the people around us for approval as well. The feeling that we are valued by them is the basis of our self-esteem.

Even when we are babies, the way our parents behave toward us is important for our self-esteem.

Family matters

Experts agree that our family helps form our vision of ourselves, particularly when we are babies and young children. Parents who talk to their children respectfully, praise their children, and show them how loved they are, will help their children develop good feelings about themselves.

Even as we grow up, the way our parents behave toward us affects our self-esteem. We feel better about ourselves if our parents are supportive of our goals and proud of our achievements. It helps if parents or guardians give us some control over our lives and choices.

We may inherit our self-esteem, in part, through our genes. Studies of twins have shown that they are often alike in their self-esteem, whether it is high or low, even if they have been separated at birth and brought up by different parents. Scientists are studying this further in order to learn whether or not there is a gene that affects our self-esteem.

Comparisons

When we go to school, we meet friends and teachers who also influence the way we feel about ourselves. We may start to compare ourselves with other children who we feel are somehow "better" than we are—smarter or better-looking. Our academic abilities are also compared through tests.

It's your opinion

Some studies have shown that girls are likely to have slightly lower self-esteem than boys. The gap is widest when they are in their late teens. Do you think that boys have naturally higher self-esteem than girls? If so, why do you think this is?

▲ Teenage girls often feel pressured to look good.

People and events

As we become adults, our self-esteem is affected by people we meet and by events in our lives. We are constantly judging ourselves, often in comparison with others. The way we feel about ourselves does not stay the same—it changes as our lives change.

If we are successful at school or work and meet people who love and value us, we feel good. If a relationship goes wrong, or if we fail an important exam, we can feel bad. Good friends can help us maintain our self-esteem at times like these. But people who don't make us feel good about ourselves are best avoided.

It's your decision

Are you too competitive?
How you feel about yourself can depend on how you compare yourself with others. But this can make us too competitive, which can lead to unhappiness if we feel we fail to measure up. We need to be careful not to become so competitive that we undermine our self-esteem—or someone else's.

As we get older, the ▶ opinions of our friends become as important to us as those of our family.

11

Measuring self-esteem

Our self-esteem is based not only on standards set by family and friends but also on those set by the community and culture we live in. These standards vary within communities, ethnic groups, and cultures.

We may look up to glamorous movie stars and measure our success against theirs—but they, too, enjoy boosts to their self-esteem through award ceremonies such as the Oscars, shown here.

Celebrity culture

In Western cultures, the lifestyles of pop stars, movie stars, models, and athletes are celebrated. Many people long to be thin, good-looking, and wealthy, living in expensive homes just like these famous people. If we live in a Western culture, our self-esteem may be partly based on how we see ourselves in relation to these ideals—whether or not we "measure up." We are encouraged to be competitive and to value individual success and wealth.

It's your opinion

Should we base our self-esteem on how we measure up to cultural ideals such as good looks and wealth? What do we risk if we do this? What makes a successful person?

Community values

In contrast, many non-Western cultures do not place importance on individual success. They measure self-esteem in terms of how much individuals contribute to the family or community around them. Even physical ideals may be different from Western models; for example, in parts of Africa, being thin is seen as a sign of poverty, so it's desirable to be plump or overweight.

Gender and age

In some cultures, such as in China, Japan, and India, boys are valued more highly than girls are because they are seen as bringing wealth and security to a family, while girls cost the family money in marriage arrangements.

Our age may also influence the way we feel about ourselves, depending on the values of the culture we live in. Western

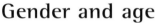 The Sikh culture emphasizes involvement in the community. Here, Sikh women volunteer to cook at their local temple.

cultures worship youth, so many older people feel left out and undervalued. But many Asian and African cultures respect and value the wisdom and understanding that comes with old age. Older people in these societies are more likely to feel valued.

Grandparents in Japan play an active part in family life and are valued for the experience age brings.

It's your experience

"My brother is really good at sports—sports captain for his grade and all that. I've never been good at sports, and I can't help feeling I am letting my family down—Dad was a good sportsman too."

Giles, age 15

13

High self-esteem

Self-esteem is an important part of our health and well-being. If we feel good about ourselves, we are more likely to take care of ourselves by making sensible choices, such as eating a balanced diet and avoiding smoking and drugs. We will have the confidence to make good decisions. Self-esteem also helps us get through difficult or stressful times and events in our lives.

Knowing our own mind

Self-esteem is all about valuing ourselves. It means we are less likely to go along with our friends if they are doing something stupid or dangerous—such as joyriding or taking drugs. By knowing our own mind, we can be confident enough to make our own decisions, even if others are trying to persuade us to do otherwise.

Dealing with problems

We all have to deal with problems at some time in our lives. These problems can make us doubt ourselves. But if we have a healthy sense of inner-self, we are less affected by criticism or rejection and are able to bounce back more easily. We know our own strengths, no matter what others say or do.

▼ If we are lucky enough to have good friends, they can support and raise our self-esteem.

Sophie's 18th birthday

It's your experience

"My family set their hearts on me becoming a doctor, but I have known right from the start that it wasn't right for me. I want to be an actress—I know it's going to be really hard, but I have to try."

Aleema, age 19

▲ Our ability to get over and learn from our failures, such as failing a driving test, is determined by our self-esteem.

▲ When we become adults, we have to take more responsibility for ourselves. Having high self-esteem gives us more confidence in our decisions.

Making choices

High self-esteem gives us the confidence to try new things and learn from our mistakes. It means we are open to advice and criticism, but we also have the ability to make our own choices without needing the approval of others.

People with high self-esteem are able to risk failure because they know they will be able to cope with it and even try again. But this does not mean we should have such a high opinion of ourselves that we think we never make mistakes. If we believe that, we are less likely to learn and grow with our experiences.

It's your decision

Are you prepared to take risks?
Can you laugh at yourself and not take yourself too seriously? If you are terrified of failure or of looking foolish, you may keep yourself from challenges that could help you grow.

Growing up

How we feel about ourselves changes throughout our lives. When we are growing up, our bodies start to change as we go through puberty. These changes can make us very aware of our body image. Puberty affects the way we feel, too. Hormones in our bloodstream can make us feel moody and emotional. It's an unsettling time.

Boys may anxiously await landmarks such as their first shave. If friends seem to be developing faster, they may start to worry that they are being left behind.

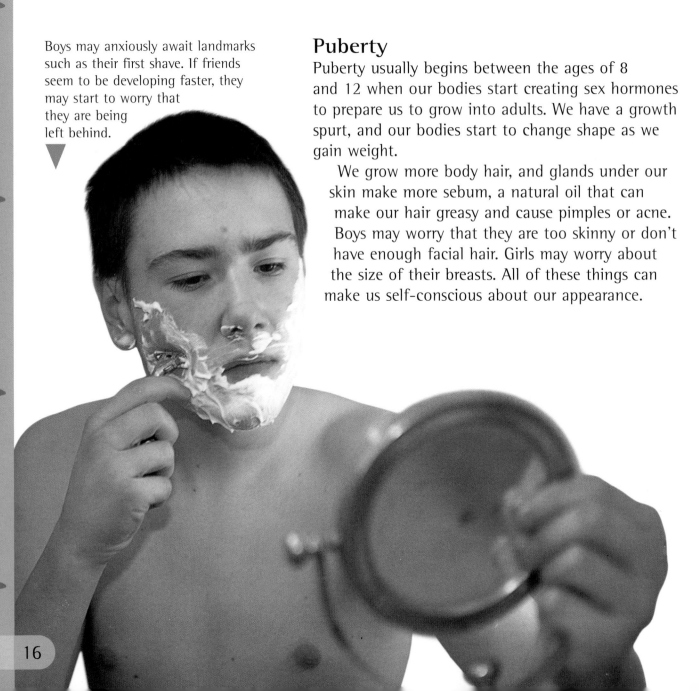

Puberty

Puberty usually begins between the ages of 8 and 12 when our bodies start creating sex hormones to prepare us to grow into adults. We have a growth spurt, and our bodies start to change shape as we gain weight.

We grow more body hair, and glands under our skin make more sebum, a natural oil that can make our hair greasy and cause pimples or acne. Boys may worry that they are too skinny or don't have enough facial hair. Girls may worry about the size of their breasts. All of these things can make us self-conscious about our appearance.

It's your decision

Can you make the best of yourself?
There are some things we can't change about ourselves, such as how tall we are. But we can make the best of the way we look through basic grooming, including keeping ourselves clean with daily showers or baths.

Teenagers can be very self-critical. Many would like to change the way they look.

Sexuality

As sex hormones start flowing through our body, we become aware of our sexuality. We start to feel sexual attraction toward others and may have fantasies about sexual partners, such as celebrities or people we know. If we approach someone we like and they show no interest in us or reject us, we are disappointed. Media images constantly tell us that we should be sexy and desirable, so if we think we fail to measure up, we can feel rejected.

Feeling different

If we find we are attracted to the same sex, we may feel that family or friends who are expecting us to be heterosexual will be disappointed. We may try to hide our sexuality. Feeling safe to honestly explore our sexuality and being able to express it in our relationships is part of our well-being.

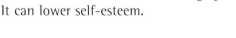
Problem skin is common in teenage years. It can lower self-esteem.

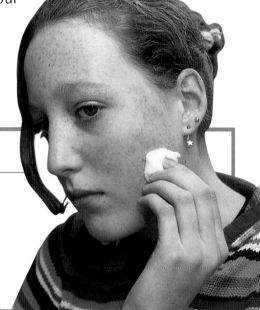

It's your experience

"My skin never really feels clean now. Having zits is a real downer when you're on a date. You feel like everyone is looking at them."

Rachel, age 15

Life events

Our self-esteem can be influenced by events in our lives. Important changes, such family or relationship breakups or coping with the death of a loved one, challenge our emotions. We can't control many of these events, but they can still affect the way we see ourselves. Making new friends or achieving success in something can make us feel good about ourselves again.

Exam results can be good or bad— can you cope with either? ▼

You win some, you lose some

As we grow up, we all need to accept the successes and failures in our lives. If your team loses a game, it is good to talk over the disappointment, but getting angry won't help.

If you feel disappointed with a class grade, talk it over with your parents or a friend or teacher. You can always do better next time. Learn to develop a range of emotional reactions to events, and keep talking to people you trust.

These relatively small events can also be useful, however, because they can help us deal with bigger crises when they arise.

It's your experience

"When my boyfriend told me he was seeing someone else, I felt like I'd been kicked in the stomach. It had been going on for ages, and I found out later that everyone seemed to know about it except me. I felt really stupid, and I also felt hurt."

Mel, age 19

Rejection

Whenever we feel rejected or hurt by others, it knocks us down. Children in foster care often have low self-esteem because they feel rejected, even though their parents may love them but cannot take care of them.

Adults have to deal with some tough situations, too, from a partner leaving or being unfaithful to losing a job or dealing with health concerns. Talking through these events and learning to forgive can help.

Family breakup

When parents break up, it can be unsettling for everyone involved. Children may have to move to a new home or school and see less of one parent. They may feel that they themselves have done something wrong. If a parent leaves home and no longer stays in touch, children may feel that they have lost that parent's love. They may begin to have problems at school, and often their schoolwork suffers. Research shows that five years after a family breakup, more than one-third of all children still feel depressed.

Bereavement

When someone close to us dies, life is very difficult because we have lost someone who made us feel good by loving and caring for us. The loss of their love leaves a gap in our lives. We may even feel guilty that we did not tell them how much we loved them, or we may feel upset about the way we behaved to them before they died.

▲ The breakup of a family is stressful and upsetting for all involved. Children may often appear to be coping, but they will be dealing with difficult feelings, and their home and school lives may suffer.

Losing a loved one is difficult at any age. ▶

It's your opinion

▶ Young adults from broken families are nearly twice as likely as others to need special help, such as counseling. Why do you think this is? What do you think will help these children rebuild their inner happiness?

The effects of low self-esteem

Low self-esteem can affect every area of our lives, from our relationships and work to our health and well-being. It can lead us to stop taking care of ourselves because inside we don't feel we are worth taking care of. If we don't respect and value ourselves, we are unlikely to respect and value others, so it can affect the way we behave toward others, too.

Self-criticism

From our earliest years, we look for approval and encouragement from those around us. So if our parents criticize us or our friends make fun of us, our self-esteem can be harmed. If we are constantly told that we are unattractive or stupid or worthless, in time we will begin to feel all those things inside. We learn to criticize ourselves and blame ourselves when things go wrong.

▲ It is natural for everyone to feel sad at times—but if the feelings don't go away, we may need to seek help.

Feeling sad

Feeling sad will make life harder to deal with and can even lead to an illness called depression (see pages 26-27). We may be afraid of trying new things because we are scared we will fail. We may compare ourselves with others who we feel are smarter and more attractive than we are. Even people who appear to us to have everything—looks, brains, and money—may feel sad inside because they don't see themselves the way others see them.

It's your decision

Do you help around the house?
Parents often nag their children to clean their bedrooms or help with the dishes. You could be doing yourself a big favor by learning how to keep your room clean and how to shop for food and prepare meals. It is a huge boost to self-confidence to know that you can help out at home, as well as live independently.

Taking risks

If we have low self-esteem, we may put our health at risk. People with low self-esteem are more likely to become addicted to tobacco, drugs, or alcohol.

We may also take risks with our sexual health by having sex before we feel ready or by failing to practice safe sex. People may stay in violent and unhappy relationships because they feel the problems are their fault or because they don't feel they deserve better.

Low expectations

Research shows that low self-esteem increases the risk of teenage pregnancy. Some girls may see pregnancy as their only means of getting social status and living independently. These girls may not see that there are other choices, such as getting more qualifications that could lead to a rewarding job and a better lifestyle.

Surveys also show a link between low self-esteem and unemployment in young men. If these men feel they are unable to compete in the job market, unemployment may seem to be a safe option.

Improve your self-esteem

Select 10 words from the box that reflect your own qualities and display a list of them in a prominent place:

adventurous	free	patient
affectionate	funny	persistent
alert	generous	pleasant
ambitious	gentle	polite
artistic	growing	practical
athletic	happy	punctual
brave	helpful	quiet
calm	healthy	relaxed
caring	honest	reliable
capable	hopeful	responsible
cheerful	imaginative	smart
confident	inventive	special
dependable	kind	strong
determined	likeable	tactful
easy-going	loving	thorough
energetic	modest	trusting
faithful	open-minded	warm
fit	outgoing	witty

▲ Work gives us purpose and interest, but it can feel like too much of an effort if our job prospects seem poor.

It's your opinion

The United States and Britain have some of the highest rates of teenage pregnancy in the world. What do you think are the main causes, and what could be done to reduce the numbers?

Body image

Our body image—the way we see and think about our body—is an important part of self-esteem. We may see ourselves as fat or skinny, worry that our nose is too big, or think our ears stick out too much. We may compare our body with others' bodies and be influenced by what others say about us. Being teased or bullied because of the way we look can make us feel even worse.

Media images

Experts believe that our body image is influenced by media images that tell us we have to look young and slim in order to be beautiful, desirable, or successful. This can lead to poor body image as we compare ourselves negatively with the ideals we see.

In Britain, for example, one survey showed that almost 80 percent of women think about their body shape every day, and only 1 percent of women are completely happy with their body. Other studies have shown that many girls have a poor body image by the age of 13.

Dolls like these impose Western ideals of youth and beauty on little girls.

Boys may also feel dissatisfied with the way they look—perhaps they feel they are too short or have a poor physique. Some may feel they have to exercise or take drugs such as steroids to improve their body.

We get many of our concepts about beauty from magazines and the media.

It's your experience

"I have a skin condition that makes my skin look red and scaly. I don't want to go swimming with my friends anymore—I feel like everyone is thinking 'Gross!'"

Patsy, age 16

It's your decision

Would you support a bully?
People may be teased or called names because of the way they look, but we should always remember that teasing or bullying others because of their appearance will hurt their feelings and lower their self-esteem.

Healthy body image

Most of us have something we would like to change about our bodies, but we all have some good features. Having a healthy body image means accepting the things we can't change about ourselves and learning how to make the most of our best features.

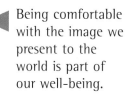

Being comfortable with the image we present to the world is part of our well-being.

Problems and changes

Unfortunately, an accident or illness can change our appearance. If we are physically scarred or left with a disability, we may become self-conscious about the way we look. We may need help from counselors or psychiatrists to achieve a feeling of acceptance about how we now look.

Eating disorders

Low self-esteem, based on poor body image, has been linked with eating disorders including anorexia nervosa and bulimia nervosa. Anyone can develop an eating disorder, although young women are most at risk.

Widespread problem

Some estimates suggest that up to 1 million men and boys and 10 million women and girls in the U.S. suffer from some form of eating disorder. In Britain, about 165,000 people are affected—1 in 10 of them are male. There have been some cases of anorexia nervosa in children as young as three.

Different types

There are several types of eating disorders. People who have anorexia nervosa will starve themselves of food and drink, often skipping meals and pretending to others that they have eaten. When people have bulimia nervosa, they will binge eat, often in secret, then make themselves vomit to get rid of the food so they won't gain weight.

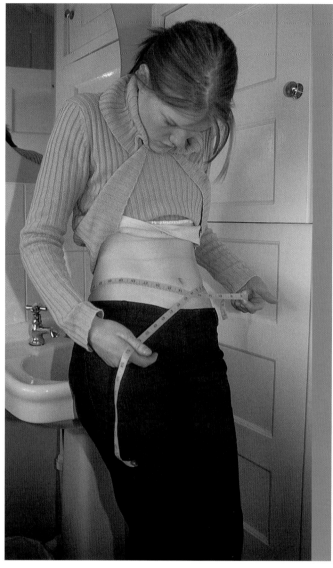

An eating disorder such as anorexia makes sufferers obsess about their size and weight.

Anorexics and bulimics see themselves as fat even when they are dangerously thin or close to death.

Binge eating—eating much more food than the body needs, often in secret and without feeling hungry—is itself an eating disorder. It can harm your body and lead to obesity.

It's your experience

"When you have an eating disorder, you don't see yourself as others see you. You can be skin and bones, and you still think you look fat."

Belinda, age 15 (recovering anorexic)

Bulimia often results in feelings of guilt and self-disgust.

Emotional problems and causes

Eating disorders may be a way of trying to cope with emotional problems or other difficulties. Sometimes they can be triggered by stressful events such as bereavement, bullying, or abuse. The eating disorder is a way of trying to block out painful feelings or gain total control over body weight when everything else in life seems out of control.

Some experts believe that eating disorders may be influenced by our genes or by a parent or guardian's attitude toward food. Others have blamed the rise in cases of eating disorders on the images of super-thin models promoted by the fashion and advertising industries.

Binge eaters often choose fatty snacks such as fries and ice cream for "comfort food."

Physical treatment

Eating disorders can lead to great unhappiness and even premature death. In cases of dangerous weight loss or weight gain, a patient will often be hospitalized. A range of treatments, including drugs and surgery, are used to help the body recover. There are continual advances in the treatment of eating disorders.

Treating underlying problems

Treatment for all eating disorders involves trying to identify and deal with the individual's underlying problem. Is food, or lack of it, filling an emotional gap in the person's life, or has something traumatic happened to him or her? Health professionals can help patients understand why they feel this way and reach a more realistic view of their appearance.

It's your opinion

Experts have criticized the fashion industry for promoting images of underweight models. Do you think these images can encourage dieting and lead to eating disorders?

Depression

Low self-esteem can sometimes be part of an illness called depression. We all feel sad at times, but when these feelings stay with us for a long time and nothing lifts our mood, we may be suffering from depression. Depression affects about 1 in 20 of us at some time in our lives. Often, "high achievers" who set high standards and goals for themselves suffer from this illness.

Brain scans show changes in chemical activity in the brain when someone is depressed.

Symptoms

People who feel depressed may feel sad and tearful much of the time. They feel down about themselves and their lives, and they cannot see any way to make things better. They may lose interest in their friends, hobbies, and even food. They may also sleep a lot or sleep badly, feel tired, and have no energy.

Normal   Depressed

It's your decision

What do you want from your life? Studies show that when children believe money, fame, and beauty can bring happiness, they are more likely to suffer from depression. It's worth remembering that even people who seem to "have it all" can suffer from depression. Research has shown that once the basic costs of living are covered, there is no strong link between the level of happiness and the amount of money an individual has.

Causes

Scientists think that the way we feel is the result of changes to chemicals in our brain called neurotransmitters. These chemicals affect our mood by stimulating our brain cells. Because depression can run in families, scientists think there may be a gene that influences these brain chemicals and makes some people more likely to become depressed than others.

Depression can be triggered by events or changes in our lives, such as the death of someone close to us. It is normal to feel devastated by such events, and depression triggered in this way usually heals itself over a period of a few months.

Antidepressant drugs may help someone through a difficult time.

It's your experience

"I didn't realize how unsettled I was going to feel when we moved to be nearer to Dad's new job. I'd left my life behind, and I felt really low and bad-tempered with everyone for several months. Now I am taking up some of the things I enjoy doing again, so I've started swimming on a team, and I'm getting to know a few people."

Sam, age 14

Treatment

When depression is lasting, it becomes an illness that needs treatment. Doctors may prescribe drugs called antidepressants. These drugs work by increasing the levels of important neurotransmitters, such as serotonin, in the brain. Because they are often addictive, doctors limit the period of time that a person takes these drugs. The underlying causes of depression also need to be treated, often with some form of therapy.

Talking about problems with a counselor can give us an insight into why we feel the way we do.

Children and depression

People often think of depression as an illness that affects only adults, but children as young as seven have been given antidepressants, and there are reports that five percent of children in the U.S. suffer from depression, often triggered by family breakdown.

It's your decision

What can you do to make yourself feel good? Many young people feel like they are on a roller coaster of emotions. Some experts think it helps to take walks through the woods or by the sea, which may restore a sense of wonder in the world. It helps to remember what makes you feel good, whether that is rollerblading or drawing, and do much more of it.

Self-harm

Sometimes, low self-esteem and depression can lead us to deliberately harm or injure our own body by cutting or burning our skin, pulling out our hair, or poisoning our body with drugs. Self-harm is always a sign of unhappiness and low self-esteem.

Physical scars, such as cuts to the arms, are an outward display of inward unhappiness.

Hurting yourself

Some people deliberately cut or burn themselves as a way of dealing with difficult feelings. People who harm themselves may be feeling trapped and helpless about a problem they cannot solve. Hurting themselves is a way of feeling in control.

The physical pain of the cut distracts them from the inner mental pain. In some instances, they may be coping with painful feelings about something that has happened to them, or they may be punishing themselves because they feel guilty or ashamed about something they have done.

Teenagers who harm themselves may be trying to cope with loss and abuse, or they may be coming to terms with their sexuality. They may be under pressure at school or at home, or perhaps they are having problems with family or friends.

Getting help

People who hurt themselves often do it secretly and feel too embarrassed and ashamed to tell others about their problem. If they are cutting or burning their skin, they may cover up the scars with long sleeves to keep their secret hidden. They need to get help because they are putting their health at risk. Scars may be lasting and can lead to blood poisoning and infections.

A recent survey discovered that 50 percent of the young people interviewed had tried to seek help before they hurt themselves. Some people will need help from a specialist such as a phychologist or a youth counselor.

Substance abuse

Abusing drugs and other harmful substances can be another symptom of deliberate self-harm. Smoking, drinking too much alcohol, and taking drugs can all harm our health. Smoking damages our lungs and can cause heart disease and cancer.

▲ Alcoholism can lead to the loss of our health, job, and home.

Drinking heavily, especially binge drinking, can lead to problems, including heart and liver disease. Drugs can damage our physical and mental health.

All of these substances are addictive, so our mind and body can come to depend on them. If we value and respect ourselves, we will avoid risking our health and well-being.

Even "soft" drug use, such as smoking marijuana, can be a sign that someone is trying to escape his or her problems. If these problems are not solved, the person may go on to try other drugs. ▶

It's your opinion

Surveys show that more teenage girls than boys harm themselves—and that self-harm is also more common in young children living in one-parent families. Why might these groups be most at risk?

Bullying and abuse

Bullying, abuse, and peer pressure can make us feel desperate about our lives. It is hard to stand our ground when someone is bullying or abusing us or when our peers are trying to persuade us to do something we don't want to do. Bullying happens to almost all of us at some point in our lives. We owe it to ourselves to try to sort out the situation so that the bullying stops.

Actor Tom Cruise has spoken openly about being the victim of bullying at school. ▼

Bullying

Bullying can be verbal, such as calling people names or insulting or threatening them. It can also be physical, such as hitting or pushing people around. People who are being bullied might feel unhappy and afraid. They may be ashamed that they are unable to stand up to the bully.

Bullies may appear confident, but this can be an act. Bullying may be their only way to get status within their peer group. Sometimes they are being bullied themselves and decide to take their feelings out on others.

Bullying can start at a young age and can make life miserable for the victim. ▶

It's your opinion

It is easy for adults or older brothers or sisters to correct, criticize, or even bully the younger members of the family. Often, people hardly realize they are doing it, yet it can be very damaging to a young person's self-esteem. Have you ever behaved in this way? Can you think of other ways to communicate?

NO ONE DESERVES TO BE BULLIED

If you are being bullied at school, follow your school's anti-bullying policy. If your school doesn't have a policy, try some of these tips:

- Tell a friend—it is harder for a bully to stand up to two people.
- Try to ignore the comments. The bully is looking for a reaction—if you don't give one, the bully may get bored.
- Don't fight back—most bullies are bigger than the person they are picking on, and you could end up making the situation worse or being blamed for it.
- Try to think of clever responses in advance, or try to make a joke of it all.
- Keep a record so that an adult can see how often you are being bullied.

Peer pressure

Sometimes our friends, or peers, may try to persuade us to do something we don't really want to do. This is called "peer pressure." If our self-esteem is low, we may give in to peer pressure because we want to fit in. We are not confident enough in our own ideas and views, so we go along with the crowd.

High self-esteem helps us resist peer pressure. We have enough self-confidence to make our own decisions and stick to them even if it means that others might dislike us or make fun of us.

It's your experience

"I got in with a crowd that was always skipping class and ditching school. I didn't really want to because I was getting really behind with schoolwork, but they gave me such grief if I said no that it was just easier to go along with it."

Todd, age 16

Abuse

When one person abuses another, he or she does or says things to the other person that make that person feel unhappy and uncomfortable. Sexual abuse means touching someone in a sexual way when he or she does not want to be touched. Sexual abuse can make victims feel ashamed because they might think that the abuse is their fault, but this is never the case.

Domestic violence is another form of abuse that takes place at home when one person hits, punches, or physically hurts another. The abuser could be a parent or a brother or sister. Any form of abuse is wrong and has to be stopped.

Some women need to find a safe house or refuge to escape abuse by partners. ▶

Community life

Self-esteem affects society as well as individuals. A nation's self-esteem can be boosted by a big sports win. The self-esteem of a town or city, a street, or an apartment complex can be boosted by community events or awards—or damaged by social problems such as vandalism, graffiti, or gun and gang crime.

When Brazil won the soccer World Cup in 2002, the nation came together to party. ▼

Antisocial behavior

Some experts blame low self-esteem for rising rates of crime, such as graffiti, burglaries, and vandalism, and other antisocial behavior, such as littering and noise pollution. They argue that if individuals don't have respect for themselves, they won't respect others or their property either. In the U.S., some communities have developed social policies to improve self-esteem because they believe it can act as a "social vaccine," protecting society against antisocial and destructive behavior.

◀ Litter is a sign that we don't care about our environment or the people who live in it.

Truancy

Children with low self-esteem are more likely to be truant from school. They may be facing problems at home, with their schoolwork, or with bullying. Skipping school can also be a way of trying to win status and approval from peers. In Britain, for example, an estimated 7.5 million school days are missed each year because of truancy. This can lead to poor education and qualifications and also increases the risk that crime and antisocial behavior will be committed by these young people while skipping school.

These young people are learning DJ skills through a youth project. ▶

Community events

Some people are fortunate enough to live in areas where there is a lot going on. Young people can join youth groups, drama clubs, music and dance groups, sports teams, or scouts—most of which are run by adults who give their free time to be involved in the community.

Some governments are realizing that communities can function much better if they are given access to these kinds of opportunities. Projects in which people are given access to sports facilities or community theater or art projects can create links across different age groups.

Get involved if you see or hear about projects like this in your area—you'll make new friends, and it can boost your self-confidence, especially when you discover you have hidden talents.

It's your opinion

While some experts believe that low self-esteem causes many social problems, others argue that there is no evidence of a link—and that people who show antisocial behavior are more likely to have such high self-esteem that they feel fearless and take risks. Which do you think is true?

It's your decision

Do you respect your community? We can all help improve our community by treating our neighbors well and taking care of the environment. By picking up garbage, being kind to neighbors, and being considerate of others when enjoying ourselves (for example, by keeping the noise down), we will make people feel more positive about us and our community.

Boosting self-esteem

Studies show that low self-esteem is linked to poor health and well-being, as well as to social problems. This has led to the introduction of courses, workshops, and social policies designed to improve self-esteem. A self-esteem industry has grown up, offering everything from guided courses, counseling, and group therapy to self-help books and CDs.

Adventure training courses teach physical skills, which in turn boost feelings of confidence and self-worth.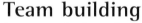

Team building

Courses designed to improve self-esteem often include team-building exercises in which people learn to work together to achieve a shared goal. Exercises such as one person leading another, blindfolded, over an obstacle are designed to build a feeling of trust, which is an important part of our relationships with others. Some may find that they have leadership skills and can encourage others to pull together as part of a team. Others learn that they are a team player, working well alongside others. This knowledge about ourselves can be carried back to school or work to help us perform at our best.

New challenges

Outward-bound or adventure camps and courses are also used to build self-esteem. These courses often include physical challenges, such as obstacle courses or survival exercises in mountains or forests. The idea is to set new challenges that stretch our skills and stamina. By achieving difficult goals, we learn that we are capable of more than we expected.

Counseling and classes

Some classes for individuals or groups offer advice and exercises to encourage positive thinking. This can include practical exercises, such as making a bulletin board or collage that reminds us of happy experiences, compliments, or feedback we have received. They may suggest thoughts or statements to repeat every day to train our minds to think positively about ourselves. Drama and role-playing may be used to help us express how we feel about ourselves and our lives.

▲ Special courses, such as this boxing class, aim to boost the self-esteem of children who have been bullied.

It's your experience

"Last summer, we went on this outward - bound course. I was terrified at first—I've never been very athletic, and I thought I was going to be an embarrassment. But the leaders were great, and they encouraged us to try everything. I felt really good about myself when I had done it."

Jamie, age 17

Schools

Schools play a huge part in most children's lives. Many schools are adopting programs intended to increase the sense of well-being in their students. Some teachers have students do exercises especially designed to improve their self-image by encouraging them to see all of the positive things about themselves. Other teachers strive to notice something that a student is good at—whether art, music, sports, or math—and suggest ways the student could get involved in activities related to that talent.

It's your opinion

Do you think activity-style self-esteem courses are good for everyone? Could they make matters worse for some people?

 ### Success every day

Think about the successes you have experienced throughout the day, and try to share them with someone. You might find this difficult at first, but you will soon realize that you have learned something or done something that amounts to a success.

Health and well-being

Self-esteem is part of our general health and well-being. If we value ourselves, we are more likely to look after our health and make sensible choices. This includes thinking carefully about what we eat, getting plenty of exercise and sleep, and avoiding health risks.

▲ Personal grooming is one outward sign that we care about ourselves.

Diet

In countries such as France and Italy, many families still sit down to enjoy meals together. They share stories about the day and discuss what is going on in each other's lives. In other countries, more people now "graze," or eat junk foods at different times of the day. Often, these junk foods are high in fat, sugar, or salt and low in healthy nutrients and vitamins.

To avoid the short bursts of energy that sweet or fatty foods give our bodies, we need to eat a balanced diet, with plenty of fresh fruits and vegetables. These foods provide us with the vitamins and minerals we need and improve our well-being and energy levels. Eating them will help us stay healthy and active.

Many people enjoy eating chocolate because it is high in fat and sugar and can give the body a "feel-good" kick. But 40 minutes later, we may start to crave more. Try to eat healthier snacks, such as fruits or a handful of nuts, which don't have this effect. ▼

It's your decision

Many people once thought that getting a suntan and even smoking were good for their health. Today, we know that they can both cause aging and cancer—so it is up to us to make the right choices for our health.

▲ Martial arts classes teach physical and mental discipline and skills.

Exercise and personal hygiene

Regular exercise is important for keeping our heart and lungs strong and helps us burn off calories and stay fit. There is also evidence that exercise reduces stress and depression and lifts our mood. This is because when we exercise, the pituitary gland releases chemicals called endorphins, which make us feel good. Try to get 10 to15 minutes of moderate exercise (such as brisk walking) every day, and make time for 20 minutes of more vigorous exercise at least 3 times a week.

It is also important to wash every day and after exercise, as well as to keep your teeth and hair clean.

It's your opinion

▶ One study in the U.S. found that teenagers who don't exercise are five times more likely to take up drugs, alcohol, and crime. Why do you think this is?

Sleep

Adults who work at night are much more likely to suffer from depression. Our bodies need sleep to function properly. This can be difficult in the teenage years because our internal body clock is moving into adult mode, which means that we may not feel tired until 11 P.M. However, if we still have to get up at 6:30 A.M. to catch the school bus, we won't be getting enough sleep.

We should try to get into the habit of being kind to our bodies by relaxing with music or reading after 9 P.M. so that we will be more likely to fall asleep earlier.

▲ Sports such as pool are a good way to relax with friends and learn new skills.

Have fun

By taking up a new sport or learning how to dance or play music in a band, we can set achievable goals for ourselves, which will improve our self-esteem. We should all spend time doing the things we enjoy.

Turning your life around

All people feel unsure about themselves—how they look, how many friends they have, how smart they are—at some time in their lives. For some, it is relatively easy to change the way they feel: parents or friends can encourage a new activity or help in other ways. Others struggle, whether because their self-esteem has become really low or because their personal circumstances are difficult. Here are the stories of a few people who found ways to turn their lives around:

Coming off drugs

"I started using marijuana at the age of 12. By the time I was 13, I was using crack, and at 16, I started smoking heroin. My schoolwork started to suffer badly, and eventually my sister-in-law found some heroin under my bed and told my mother. Eventually, I checked into a drug treatment center. I like my life now better than it was. I like to be clean. I've got no worries.... I'm not looking for my next fix. Today I must admit that I'm happy that I'm finding me. My addiction is not the only thing about me."

Sanita, age 16

Getting active

"I've always been labeled 'the shy one' in my family, and I was happy with that. But now I see other people having a really interesting time on weekends and vacations. Also, my older sisters have left home, and it is really quiet with my parents. I really like being outside, so I've started going to a nature reserve on weekends to help clear trails. Because we are busy, I don't feel like I have to be talking to people all the time, but when we go in for a break, we've all got something to talk about.

I really look forward to the volunteer weekends—now I have something interesting to do on the weekend, too."

Stella, age 15

Sporting differences

"My school is well-known for soccer, and I'm not very good at it. I always get picked last in our gym class, and the teachers seem to like the soccer players better. Sometimes I'd pretend to be sick on gym class days, and I used to sit at home and wonder why I was so useless. Then my mom heard about a local basketball group, and I went along one day. It took a lot of courage to go because I thought I'd be awful at that too. The people there are really nice, and I really enjoy the coaching. I've been going for six months now, and I've just made the team! I think I am good at sports after

all—I just didn't realize, because soccer just wasn't for me."

Peter, age 15

Knowing your own mind

"I never really enjoyed going to school and was really worried about what to do when I graduate. My parents both went to college and have always been disappointed with my school grades. I used to study more and more to please them, but I never enjoyed it.

Near the end of last year, I did some work experience at a tree nursery. I really enjoyed being outdoors all day and working with my hands. I learned a lot in just one week. Now I know that when I finish school I'm going to work outdoors,

maybe at a tree nursery. My parents won't like it when I tell them, but I know this is what I want."

Sam, age 16

Positive thinking

We all talk to ourselves inside our heads, giving ourselves feedback about how we look and how well or badly we have done. If we are constantly putting ourselves down, we will feel bad about ourselves. By focusing on our successes and complimenting ourselves when we have achieved something, we will increase our feelings of self-worth.

Build self-confidence

Build on your past successes. No matter how bad things may seem, you must admit that you have succeeded at times. These are the thoughts to dwell on for future growth and development.

Have fun

Before you go to bed, try listing three things that you enjoyed during the day and that made you feel good. Plan to do more tomorrow!

Banish that nasty voice

Write down the nasty things that the voice in your head says and then think of better, more encouraging things to say instead. "I didn't do very well on that exam—but I did try my best, and I think I can do better next time."

Call yourself stupid?

Do you call yourself stupid if you make a mistake? Do you call yourself a failure if you give up on a diet? If your mistakes are pointed out to you, do you feel as if you are under attack and become defensive? You're only human, so treat yourself kindly. Allow yourself to make mistakes, and laugh about them.

Replace criticism with encouragement

Encourage yourself and your friends rather than criticizing them. Give compliments or a pat on the back. Think about things positively and go for what you want.

Accept compliments

Do you interpret events and comments in a negative way? If your friend says your hair looks nice, do you think, "What was wrong with it yesterday?" Just accept the compliment and think the best of the person who gave it.

Ask for help

Never be afraid to tell people how you are feeling. Talk to your friends and family or check out one of the organizations listed on page 43.

Glossary

Abuse hurting someone by words or actions that make them feel unhappy or distressed

Addictive something that the mind and body come to need and depend on

Alcohol abuse when people drink so much alcohol that they are harming their health

Anorexia nervosa an eating disorder that makes people starve themselves of food and drink to try to lose weight

Antidepressants drugs used to prevent or treat depression

Binge drinking drinking excessive amounts of alcohol in one session—more than four drinks for a woman and five for a man

Binge eating when someone eats more food than his or her body needs, often in secret

Body image how we see our own bodies

Bulimia nervosa an eating disorder in which people binge eat, then get rid of the food by making themselves sick or using drugs that make them go to the bathroom

Bullying using words or actions to make people feel afraid or to make them do something they don't want to do

Depression when someone feels down and unhappy and the feelings don't go away

Domestic violence violence in the home—when one person physically hurts another

Drug abuse using illegal drugs such as marijuana, heroin, or cocaine for recreational purposes

Gene part of the makeup of our bodies and minds that we inherit from our parents

Hormone a chemical made in our bodies that circulates through our bloodstream

Neurotransmitter a chemical in the brain that stimulates the brain cells

Nutrient part of food that we need to keep our bodies healthy

Obesity being seriously overweight: with a body mass index of more than 30 (body mass index = weight in pounds ÷ height in inches squared x 703)

Peer pressure when friends our age try to make us do something or behave in a certain way

Pituitary gland a gland that releases chemicals that control how our body grows and matures

Psychiatrist a medical expert who studies mental and emotional problems

Psychologist a medical expert who studies our minds and behavior

Puberty the time when our body changes to make us capable of having babies

Self-harm deliberately harming or injuring our bodies

Vitamins and minerals important nutrients in food that we need to stay healthy

Further information

Kids Health
Provides an internet directory of useful articles covering teen health, puberty, and other issues.

www.kidshealth.org

Eating Disorder Referral and Information Center
Provides information about eating disorders, as well as referrals to eating disorder treatment professionals.

www.edreferral.com

Bullying.org
A Web site dedicated to providing information on bullying and what you can do about it.

www.bullying.org

Palo Alto Medical Foundation
A site providing information on teenage self-esteem, depression, and anxiety.

www.pamf.org/teen/life/depression/selfesteem.html

TeensHealth
Provides practical ways to improve your self-esteem.

www.kidshealth.org/teen/your_mind/emotions/self_esteem.html

Tel-a-Teen
A Web site that enables teens to chat with other teens about the ups and downs of teen life.

www.tel-a-teen.org

Note to parents and teachers: Every effort has been made to ensure that these Web sites are suitable for children, that they are of the highest educational value, and that they contain no inappropriate or offensive material. However, because of the nature of the Internet, it is impossible to guarantee that the contents of these sites will not be altered. We strongly advise that Internet access be supervised by a responsible adult.

Index

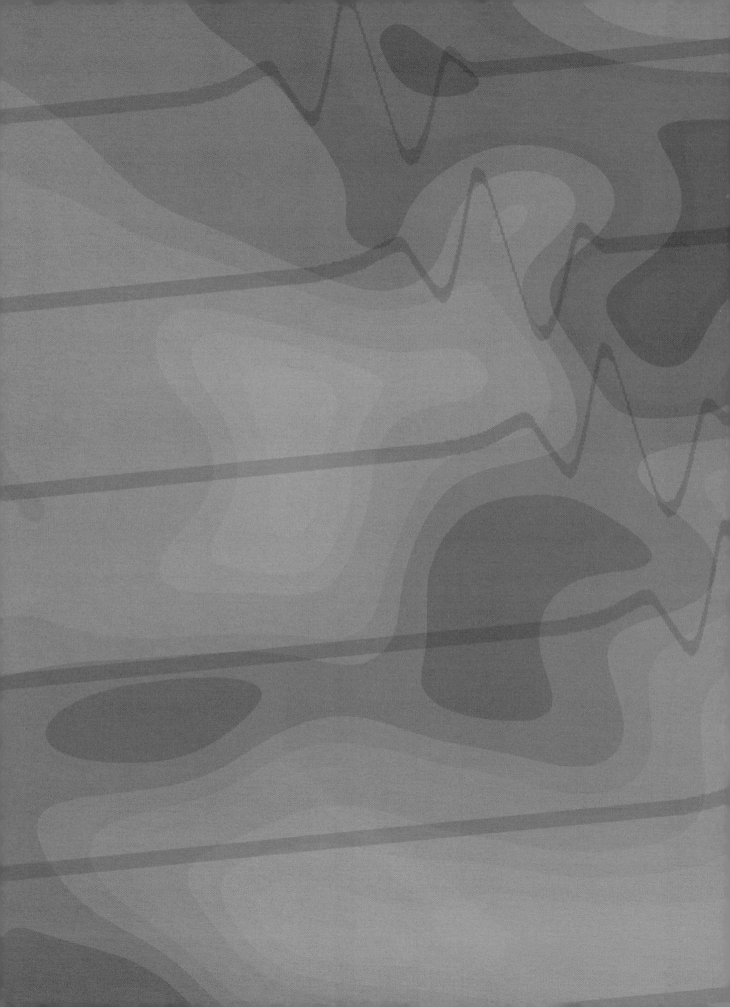